MAKING
FANTASTIC
ALIENS AND
SPACESHIPS

Design   David West
                Children's Book Design
Designer   Keith Newell
Editor   Michael Flaherty
Photography   Roger Vlitos

© Aladdin Books 1992
Designed and produced by
Aladdin Books Ltd
28 Percy Street
London W1P 9FF

First published in
Great Britain in 1992 by
Franklin Watts
96 Leonard Street
London EC2A 4RH

ISBN 0-7496-0789-0

A CIP catalogue record for this book is
available from the British Library.

Printed in Belgium

Why throw it away?

MAKING
FANTASTIC
ALIENS AND
SPACESHIPS

FRANKLIN WATTS
London: New York: Toronto: Sydney

JEN GREEN

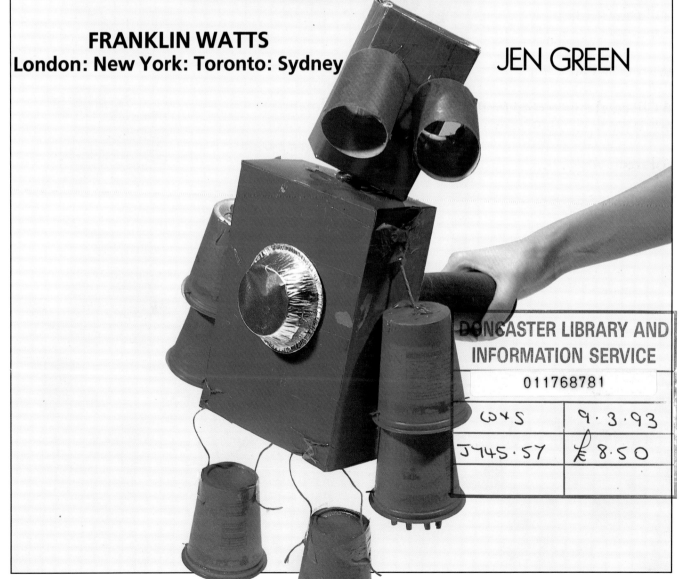

CONTENTS

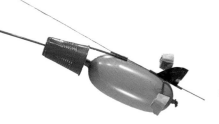

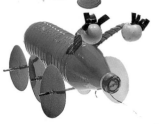

INTRODUCTION

This book will show you how to make your own collection of fantastic aliens and spaceships – toys and action models that race or fly. Each project is explained in easy stages. There are also ideas about how you can decorate the models, bringing in your own imagination.

New for old

All the models described in this book can be made from everyday junk that you and your family usually throw away. Each project provides a list of junk items that can be used to make the model. But if you haven't got one of the items suggested, don't worry; you may have something that will do just as well.

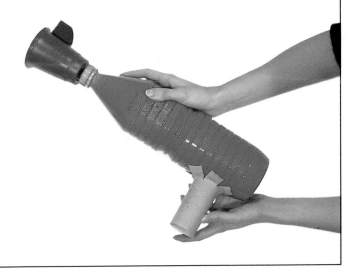

Collecting junk

Start your collection of junk materials now. Save anything that might come in handy, and ask your family to pass junk to you rather than throw it away. Make sure your materials are clean before you store them, in plastic bags or in a big cardboard box.

Balloon-powered Rocket

This simple rocket, driven by a balloon, streaks through space when its balloon is released. The rocket zooms along a string tied between two pieces of furniture.

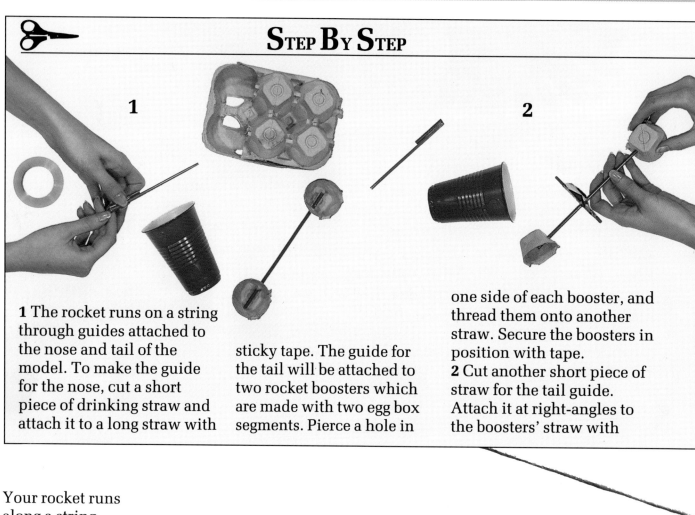

1 The rocket runs on a string through guides attached to the nose and tail of the model. To make the guide for the nose, cut a short piece of drinking straw and attach it to a long straw with sticky tape. The guide for the tail will be attached to two rocket boosters which are made with two egg box segments. Pierce a hole in one side of each booster, and thread them onto another straw. Secure the boosters in position with tape.

2 Cut another short piece of straw for the tail guide. Attach it at right-angles to the boosters' straw with

Your rocket runs along a string anchored between two pieces of furniture. Tie one end of a long piece of string to one anchor point. Thread the other end through the straws on the nose and tail of the rocket. Stretch the string taut and tie it to your second anchor point.

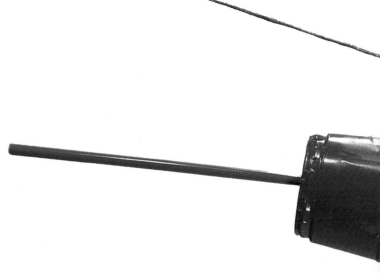

egg box

balloon

scissors

string

sticky tape

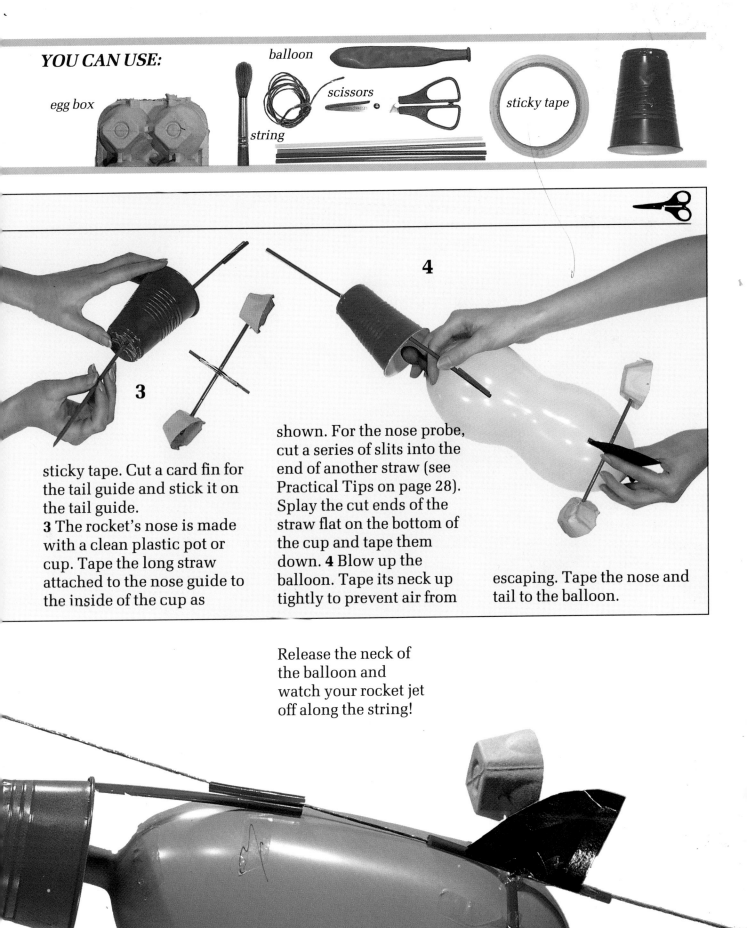

3

4

sticky tape. Cut a card fin for the tail guide and stick it on the tail guide.

3 The rocket's nose is made with a clean plastic pot or cup. Tape the long straw attached to the nose guide to the inside of the cup as

shown. For the nose probe, cut a series of slits into the end of another straw (see Practical Tips on page 28). Splay the cut ends of the straw flat on the bottom of the cup and tape them down. **4** Blow up the balloon. Tape its neck up tightly to prevent air from

escaping. Tape the nose and tail to the balloon.

Release the neck of the balloon and watch your rocket jet off along the string!

WRIST COMMUNICATOR

No sounds can travel through space, but you can keep in touch with fellow astronauts or with base control with the help of this radio communicator.

You could also use buttons, plastic bottle tops, or toothpaste tube caps to make knobs for your control panel.

You will be able to pull out and push in the aerial if you pierce a hole for it through the control panel and the bracelet. Push the aerial into the hole, and wrap sticky tape around the end inside the bracelet so that it does not drop out.

1 Cut the bracelet from the middle section of a plastic bottle. To make the bracelet

tin foil

two toilet roll tubes

drinking straw

plastic bottle

STEP BY STEP

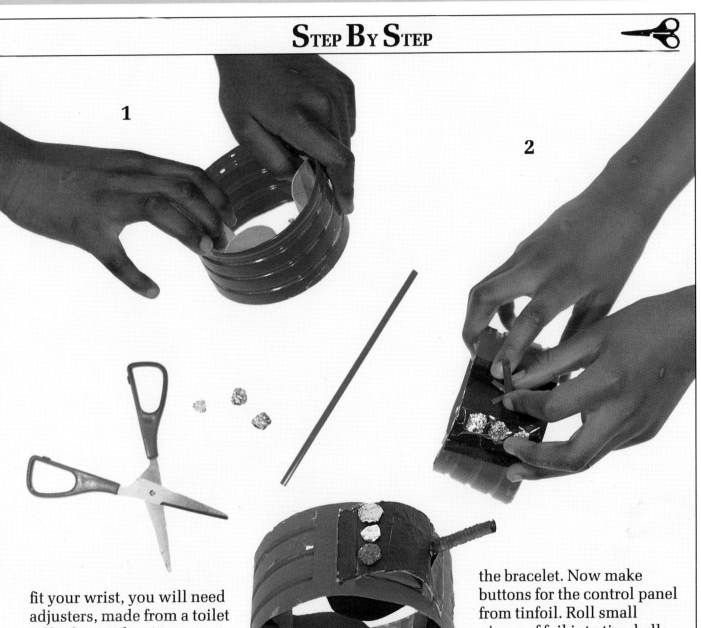

1

2

fit your wrist, you will need adjusters, made from a toilet roll tube. With scissors, cut the tube in half lengthways and then widthways, to form four sections. Fold the edges of the sections back to make flaps. Tape the flaps round the inside of the bracelet. Try the bracelet on and add or take away adjusters until it fits. **2** The control panel of the communicator is made with a quarter section cut from another toilet roll tube. Fold the edges back to make flaps and tape it to the outside of the bracelet. Now make buttons for the control panel from tinfoil. Roll small pieces of foil into tiny balls and then flatten them between your fingers. Glue or tape them to the panel. Make an aerial for your radio communicator with a drinking straw. Cut a series of slits into one end of the straw. Splay the cut ends of the straw flat onto the panel and tape them down.

ALIEN FEET

These wacky alien feet are a must for space games and fancy dress parties. The ones shown here have long, crinkly veins and brightly coloured toes.

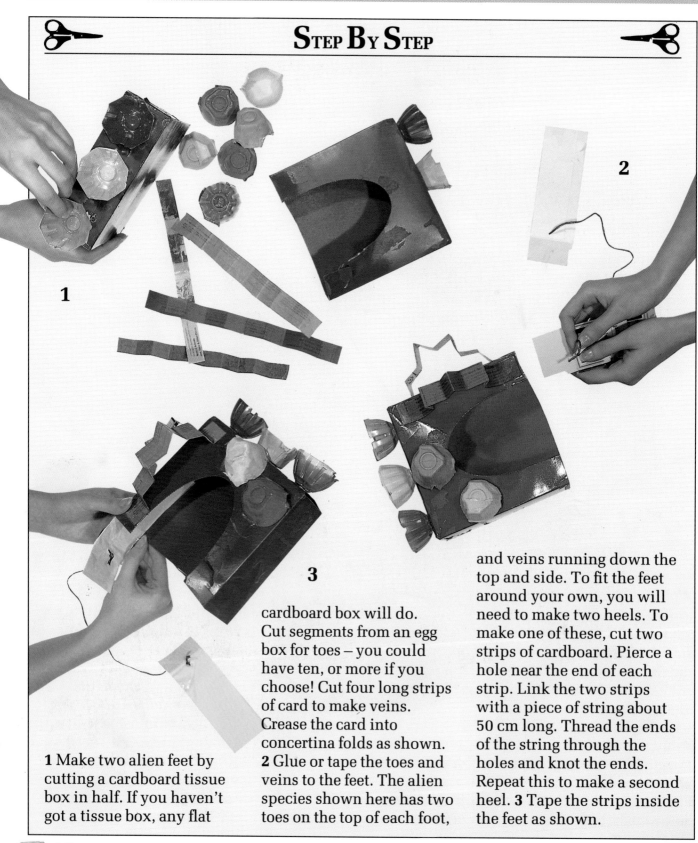

cardboard box will do. Cut segments from an egg box for toes – you could have ten, or more if you choose! Cut four long strips of card to make veins. Crease the card into concertina folds as shown. **2** Glue or tape the toes and veins to the feet. The alien species shown here has two toes on the top of each foot, and veins running down the top and side. To fit the feet around your own, you will need to make two heels. To make one of these, cut two strips of cardboard. Pierce a hole near the end of each strip. Link the two strips with a piece of string about 50 cm long. Thread the ends of the string through the holes and knot the ends. Repeat this to make a second heel. **3** Tape the strips inside the feet as shown.

1 Make two alien feet by cutting a cardboard tissue box in half. If you haven't got a tissue box, any flat

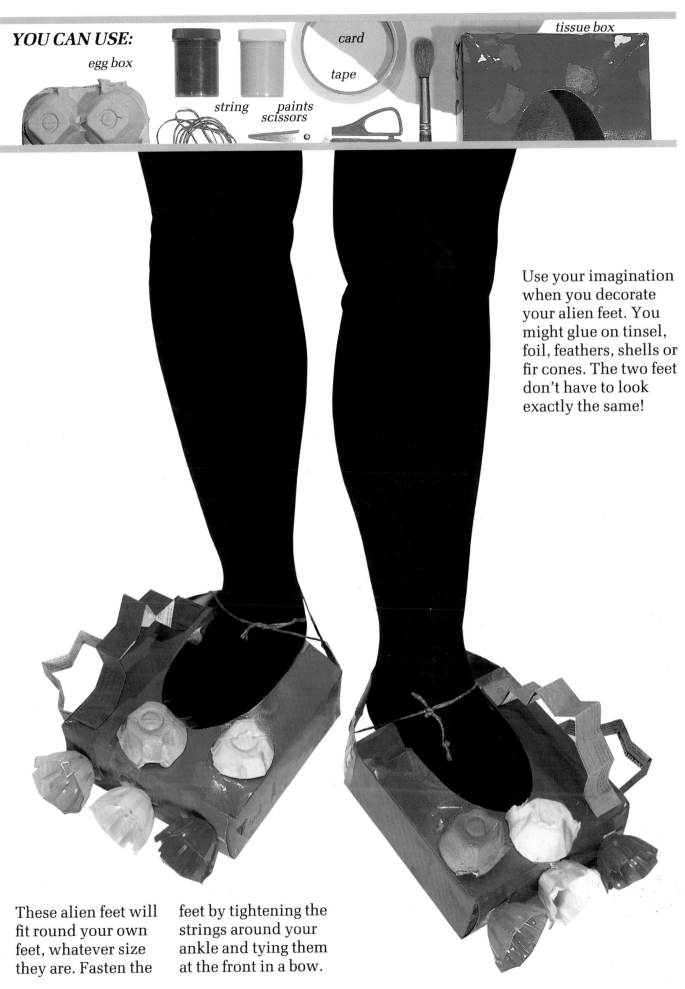

Use your imagination when you decorate your alien feet. You might glue on tinsel, foil, feathers, shells or fir cones. The two feet don't have to look exactly the same!

These alien feet will fit round your own feet, whatever size they are. Fasten the feet by tightening the strings around your ankle and tying them at the front in a bow.

11

REGGIE THE ROBOT

Reggie is a young robot and his movements can be shy and clumsy. You can control him using the handle attached to his back.

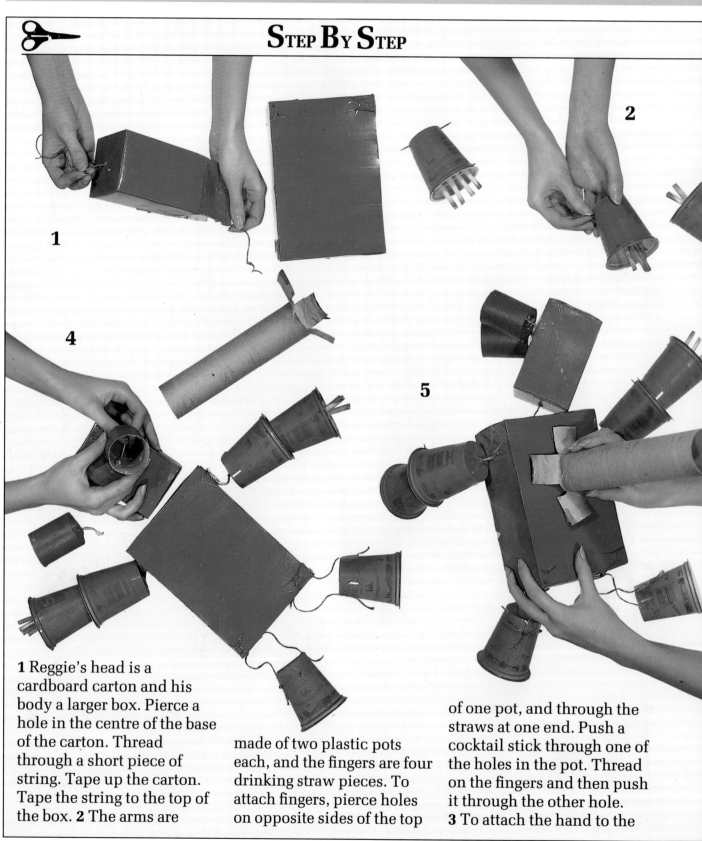

1 Reggie's head is a cardboard carton and his body a larger box. Pierce a hole in the centre of the base of the carton. Thread through a short piece of string. Tape up the carton. Tape the string to the top of the box. **2** The arms are made of two plastic pots each, and the fingers are four drinking straw pieces. To attach fingers, pierce holes on opposite sides of the top of one pot, and through the straws at one end. Push a cocktail stick through one of the holes in the pot. Thread on the fingers and then push it through the other hole. **3** To attach the hand to the

toilet roll tube

string

cardboard carton

small foil dish

3

tube. Cut slits in one end to make flaps (see page 28).
5 Splay the flaps against

Reggie's back and tape them securely.

arm, pierce holes on opposite sides of the base of the hand pot and top of another pot. Hold the hand pot inside the arm pot, and pass a cocktail stick through the holes. The hand pot hangs inside the other. To attach an arm to the body, make knots at either end of a piece of string, and tape the string in front of the knots to the arm pot and to the body. **4** Reggie's eyes are made from a toilet roll tube cut in half. Attach them to the head with short pieces of knotted string, as you did the arms. His feet are plastic pots, taped on in the same way. Use longer pieces of string, knotted and taped to both sides of each pot. Now make a control handle for the robot with a kitchen roll

You can decorate Reggie's chest with a small foil dish, or use bottle and tube tops for knobs and dials.

BUG-EYED MONSTER

This alien species has fearsome eyes which wobble as the monster is pulled along. The model is a fast, smooth runner which can be raced on any flat surface.

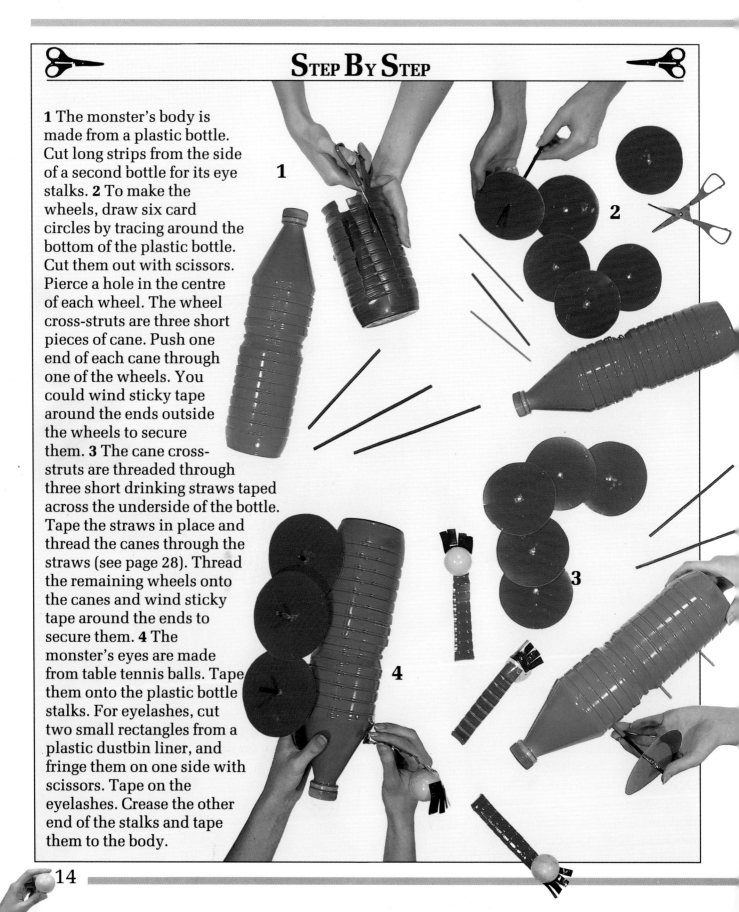

1 The monster's body is made from a plastic bottle. Cut long strips from the side of a second bottle for its eye stalks. **2** To make the wheels, draw six card circles by tracing around the bottom of the plastic bottle. Cut them out with scissors. Pierce a hole in the centre of each wheel. The wheel cross-struts are three short pieces of cane. Push one end of each cane through one of the wheels. You could wind sticky tape around the ends outside the wheels to secure them. **3** The cane cross-struts are threaded through three short drinking straws taped across the underside of the bottle. Tape the straws in place and thread the canes through the straws (see page 28). Thread the remaining wheels onto the canes and wind sticky tape around the ends to secure them. **4** The monster's eyes are made from table tennis balls. Tape them onto the plastic bottle stalks. For eyelashes, cut two small rectangles from a plastic dustbin liner, and fringe them on one side with scissors. Tape on the eyelashes. Crease the other end of the stalks and tape them to the body.

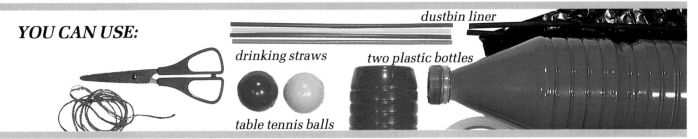

Paint your monster with bright poster colours. You could paint the body with spots or stripes.

You could attach a string to the front of the monster's body to pull it along. Or make two models with a friend, and race them down a smooth, angled surface.

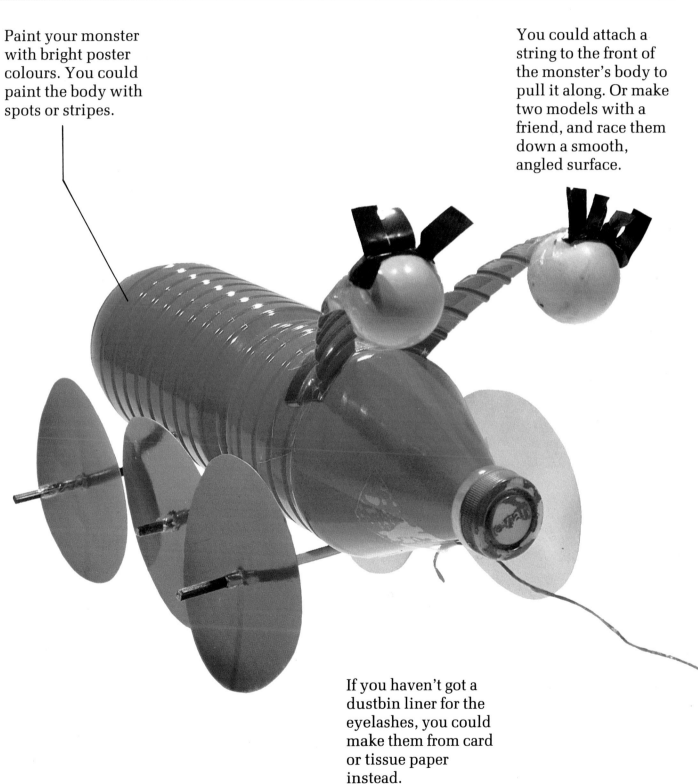

If you haven't got a dustbin liner for the eyelashes, you could make them from card or tissue paper instead.

RAY GUN & ZAPPING PISTOL

No star war would be complete without a ray gun or pistol to zap unwary aliens. But beware, the monsters you meet may fight back with weapons of their own!

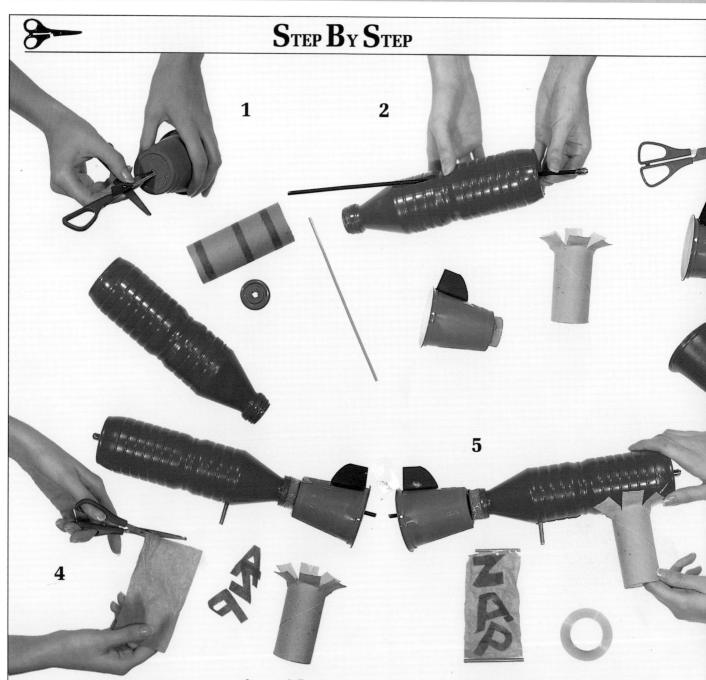

STEP BY STEP

1 For the zapping pistol's barrel and muzzle, pierce a hole through the base of a cup, and through the lid and base of a bottle. 2 For the handle, cut slits into the end of a toilet roll tube. Splay the end flat (see page 28). Cut a fin shape from card and tape it to the muzzle. Cut a trigger slot in the side of the bottle, about 5cm long and 1cm wide. Wind sticky tape around one end of a garden cane. Push the other end through the bottle's base and the trigger slot. 3 For the trigger, fold a drinking straw in half and tape it around the cane. 4 Push the cane through the neck of the bottle. Thread the bottle top onto the cane and screw it on the bottle.

plasticine

plastic cups or pots

3

6

5 Tape pieces of straw to the top and bottom of the flag. Fit the top straw over the end of the cane. Tape the handle onto the pistol.

To load the pistol, pull the trigger back with your finger. To fire it, push the trigger forward. The flag will pop from the muzzle and unfurl to zap your victim.

The ray gun (**6**) is made in the same way as the pistol, but it has no zapping mechanism. You will need a large plastic bottle and another cardboard tube to make a second handle.

Thread on the cup. For the Zap! flag use a rectangle of paper. Cut the letters from different coloured paper and glue them on.

SPACE VOYAGER MOBILE

This mobile features an astronaut on a trip around our solar system, and some of the sights he or she might expect to see on the way.

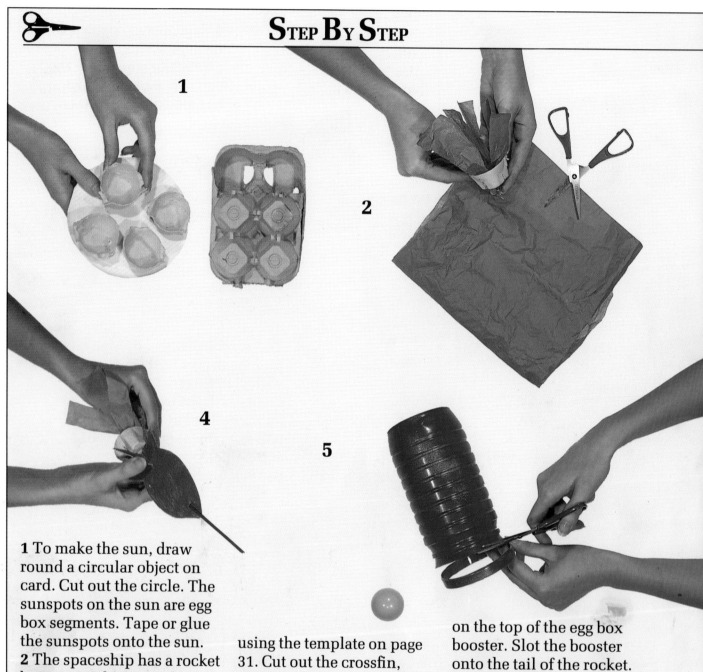

1 To make the sun, draw round a circular object on card. Cut out the circle. The sunspots on the sun are egg box segments. Tape or glue the sunspots onto the sun.
2 The spaceship has a rocket booster, with tissue paper flames. The booster is another egg box segment. Make a hole in the top of the booster, and push tissue paper strips through. Secure them with tape. 3 Cut out a card shape for the rocket,

using the template on page 31. Cut out the crossfin, using the template on page 30. Cut a slot in the tail to take the crossfin. The probe for the rocket nose is a straw cut down at an angle as shown. Glue or tape on the probe. 4 Cut four slits at right-angles to one another

on the top of the egg box booster. Slot the booster onto the tail of the rocket.
5 Use a small ball to make a planet. Cut a strip around a plastic bottle to form the planet's ring. 6 Cut shapes for the crescent moon and star from card, using the templates on pages 31. Cover them with foil of

YOU CAN USE:

paper

thread

paper clip

tinfoil

ping pong ball

garden cane

3

Attach the models to the cross-frame with cotton. Small plasticine blobs help balance the models.

Attach a large paper clip to the frame so you can hang it somewhere. Attach the frame with thread if you want it to turn freely.

6

different colours. Use the two templates on page 30 stuck back to back for the Astronaut. Make a cross-frame by tying two pieces of cane together with string.

Your mobile could feature the Earth, Mars, Venus or other planets from our solar system.

CRAZY MOONBUG

This strange species is adapted to travel in the rough craters of the moon. Its off-centre wheels make the model wobble crazily when it is pulled along.

STEP BY STEP

1 Make the moonbug's body from a clean plastic dish. Tape a drinking straw across the top of the dish. Push a piece of cane through the straw (see page 28). **2** The cane forms a cross-strut for the moonbug's back wheels, made from the lids of aerosol cans. Pierce a hole in the top of both lids for the cane to go through. The holes should be placed off-centre on each lid, to produce the moonbug's wobbling movement. Cut two small card circles for the front wheels. Make a support for the front wheel with two straws. Join the straws together by taping them in the middle and at one end. Attach the circles to this end by pushing a cocktail stick through the

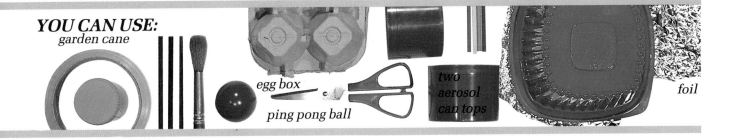

egg box

ping pong ball

two
aerosol
can tops

foil

centre of one circle, through the straws and then through the other circle. Fold the other ends of the straws back to form a T-shape.

3 Tape the T-shape to the front of the moonbug's body. Push the back wheels onto the cross-strut. Cut two egg box segments for eyes and tape them on.

Tape on a ping pong or cotton wool ball for moonbug's nose. Paint pupils in the egg box eyes.

Cut strips of tinfoil, wool or tissue paper to make hair. Tape or glue them to the moonbug's head.

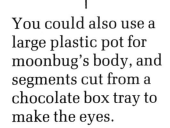

You could also use a large plastic pot for moonbug's body, and segments cut from a chocolate box tray to make the eyes.

FLYING SAUCER OUTFIT

This spectacular outfit should provide you with a passport to parties and games on planet Earth and throughout the universe.

STEP BY STEP

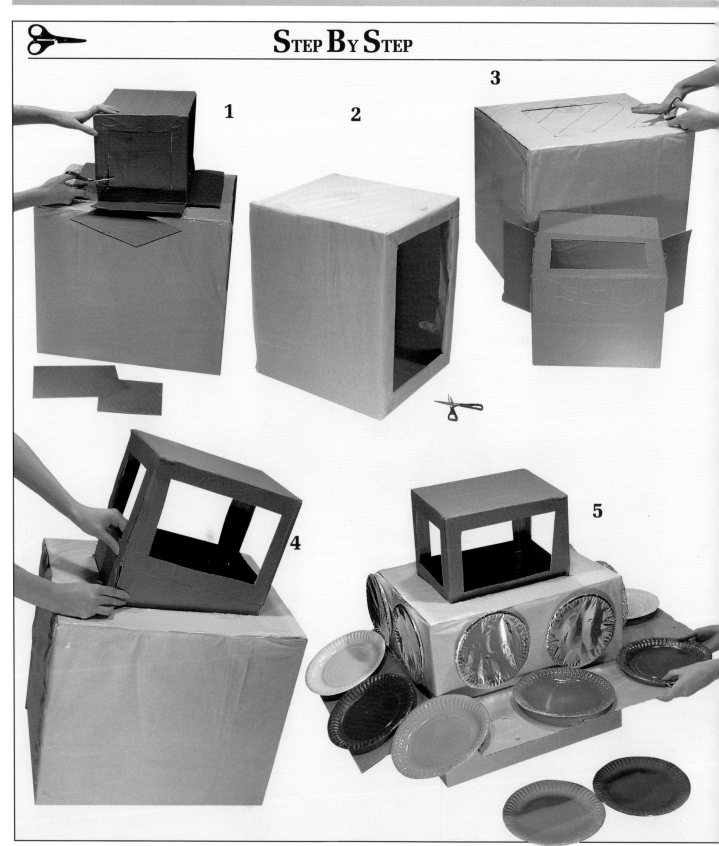

1

2

3

4

5

YOU CAN USE:

plastic bottles

box

drinking straw

foil

paper plates

1 To make the flying saucer outfit you will need a big cardboard box for the body and a smaller one for the head. Mark a large square inside each of the four sides on the small box. Cut the squares out with scissors.
2 Mark a large square on the bottom of the big box and cut it out. **3** Close the small box and place it on top of the big one. Mark round the small box with a pen and cut out the square that you have drawn on the big box. **4** Open the flaps of the small box and push them through the neck hole you made in the big box.

Tape the flaps of the small box flat inside the top of the big box. **5** Now build the saucer shape around the body, using large flaps of cardboard cut from another box. Fold the flaps around the body as shown, and tape them on. Tape cardboard struts under the flaps if you want them to stick out. Decorate the saucer shape with circles of card or with paper plates.

Paint your saucer outfit with bright poster paint. You could wrap tinfoil around some of the card circles on the body. You could also cut armholes in the body if you wish.

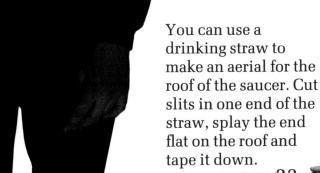

You can use a drinking straw to make an aerial for the roof of the saucer. Cut slits in one end of the straw, splay the end flat on the roof and tape it down.

23

POWERED SPACE CRAWLER

This small, menacing creature has a dynamo driven by an elastic band. Wind up the dynamo, and watch the alien creep along.

STEP BY STEP

1 Make the crawler's body by cutting two strips of dustbin liner (or black paper) about 10 x 7 cm. Fringe both strips with scissors.

2 Make the crawler's eyes by cutting a small circle of paper in half. Now begin the creature's dynamo by cutting a piece of candle about 1.5 cm long. Remove the wick from the piece of candle and enlarge the hole a little. Thread a small elastic band through the hole. You may need to hook it through using a bit of wire or a straightened paperclip.

3 Push a cocktail stick or a spent match through the loop at one end of the elastic band to secure it inside the candle. Hook the other end through a cotton reel.

4 Fasten a paperclip onto this end of the elastic band and tape the clip firmly to the side of the reel. Now straighten out two paperclips, and tape one along the top of each of the fringes you made earlier.

5 Make one end of each clip into a hook. Push the hooks into the hole in the candle, so that they sit over the cocktail

paper

elastic bands

cotton reel

cocktail stick

dustbin liner

candle

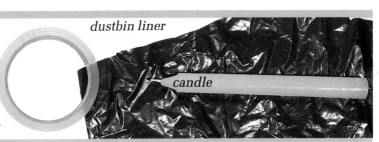

3

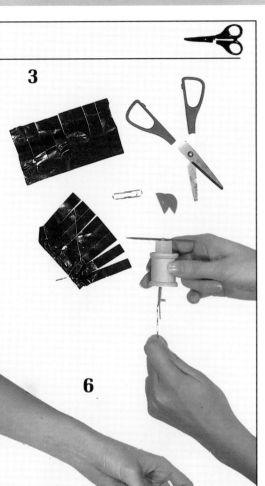

6

To wind up the crawler's dynamo, hold the candle and cocktail stick firmly in one hand and turn the cotton reel with the other hand. Give the reel a number of turns. Put the crawler down on a flat surface and watch it as it creeps along.

The crawler's cocktail stick should lift the creature up over objects placed in its path.

Make a different species of alien by using tinfoil instead of a dustbin liner to make the body.

stick. Bend the crawler's fringes around the dynamo.
6 Draw pupils on the crawler's eyes and tape them to one of the fringes.

POP-UP MOONSCAPE

Surprise your friends with this cratered moonscape, apparently devoid of life. Place the box on a flat surface, and watch three aliens shoot from the craters!

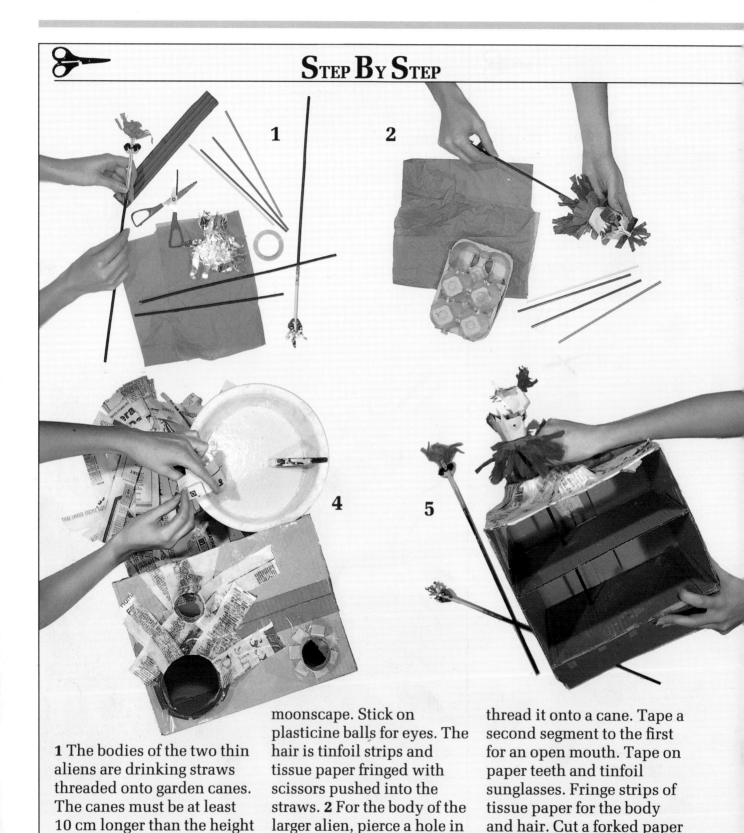

1 The bodies of the two thin aliens are drinking straws threaded onto garden canes. The canes must be at least 10 cm longer than the height of the box used for the moonscape. Stick on plasticine balls for eyes. The hair is tinfoil strips and tissue paper fringed with scissors pushed into the straws. **2** For the body of the larger alien, pierce a hole in an egg box segment and thread it onto a cane. Tape a second segment to the first for an open mouth. Tape on paper teeth and tinfoil sunglasses. Fringe strips of tissue paper for the body and hair. Cut a forked paper tongue. **3** The moonscape

cardboard box
newspaper

toilet roll tube

flour and
water paste

egg box

plastic bottle

Decorate the aliens
and moonscape with
tinfoil or bright poster
paint.

3

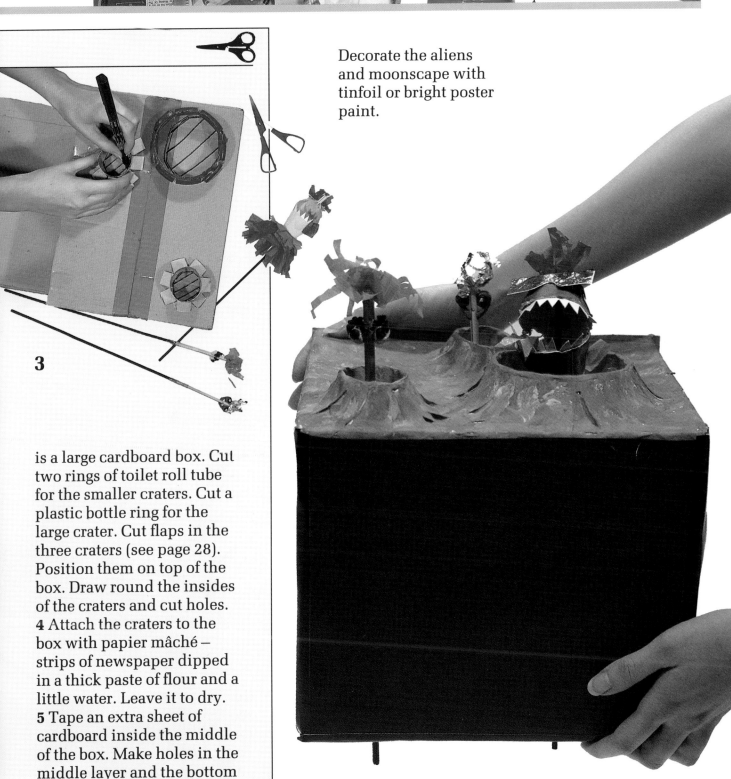

is a large cardboard box. Cut
two rings of toilet roll tube
for the smaller craters. Cut a
plastic bottle ring for the
large crater. Cut flaps in the
three craters (see page 28).
Position them on top of the
box. Draw round the insides
of the craters and cut holes.
4 Attach the craters to the
box with papier mâché –
strips of newspaper dipped
in a thick paste of flour and a
little water. Leave it to dry.
5 Tape an extra sheet of
cardboard inside the middle
of the box. Make holes in the
middle layer and the bottom
of the box below the craters.
Thread the canes through
the holes. Tape the box shut.

PRACTICAL TIPS

Below are a few practical hints to help you with some of the projects described in this book and with your model-making in general.

MAKING WHEELS

This tip will help you with all models that run on wheels, such as the moonbug on pages 20-1.

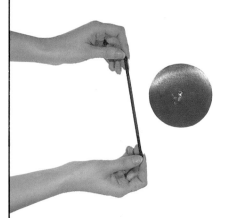

Whether your wheels are made of card or plastic, they will need a cross-strut or axle on which they can rotate freely. A cane pushed through a drinking straw makes a good axle. If you want your model to bounce along, as the moonbug does, pierce holes for the axle off-centre of your wheels.

Push the wheels onto the axle. Wind a little tape round the cane outside the wheel to secure it.

CREATING FLAPS

Use this tip for the projects on pages 8-9, 16-17, 22-23 and 26-7, and for fastening tube shapes on your models generally.

Cut a number of short slits around one end of the tube with scissors. The slits create a series of flaps. Bend

the flaps outwards. Now you will be able to press the tube flat onto the surface of your model. Attach the tube to the model with glue, sticky tape or papier mâché.

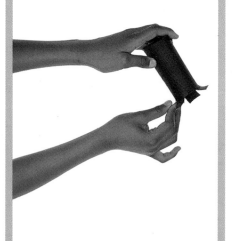

PAINTING

Poster paint, diluted with water, has been used to decorate many of the projects in this book.

To get paint to stick to plastic or tape, you could add a little washing-up liquid to your mixing water. Stir it round with your brush or with a stick to mix it well before you begin.

NATURAL MATERIALS:
twigs, leaves, petals, acorns, conkers, nuts, fir cones, bark, shells, pebbles, sponge, cork, feathers.

MORE JUNK IDEAS

The materials used most often in this book have been paper, card and plastic packaging. Below are some more suggestions about the kinds of junk which can be used to make and decorate your models.

PAPER: newspapers, comics and magazines, postcards and birthday cards, unused wallpaper, tissue.

WOOD: spent matches, garden cane, clothespegs, cotton reels, lolly sticks.

PLASTIC: food containers, sweet and crisp wrappers, buttons, broken toys.

FABRIC: wool, socks, old clothes or sheets, cloth and felt scraps.

METAL: soft drink cans, tin foil, springs, pipecleaners, coathangers, paper clips.

TEMPLATES

These templates are for you to trace to help you with some of the models made in this book. You can create your own templates very easily.

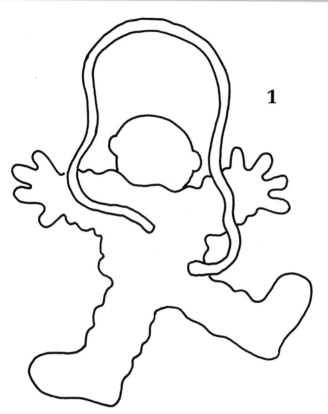

1

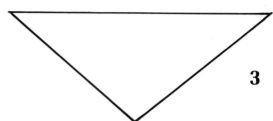

3

Use these templates to make the space voyager mobile on pages 18-19.

1,2 Astronaut
3,4 Rocket and tailfin
5,6 Crescent moon and star

To use these templates:
1 Trace the template shape onto tracing paper or thin cartridge paper.
2 Turn the tracing over, and place it on top of the paper or cardboard on which you want the image to appear. Scribble over the lines showing through the paper with your pencil. A mirror image of the template will appear on the cardboard.

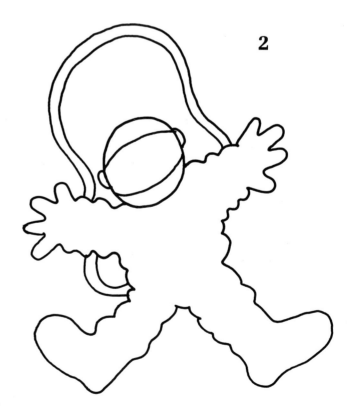

2

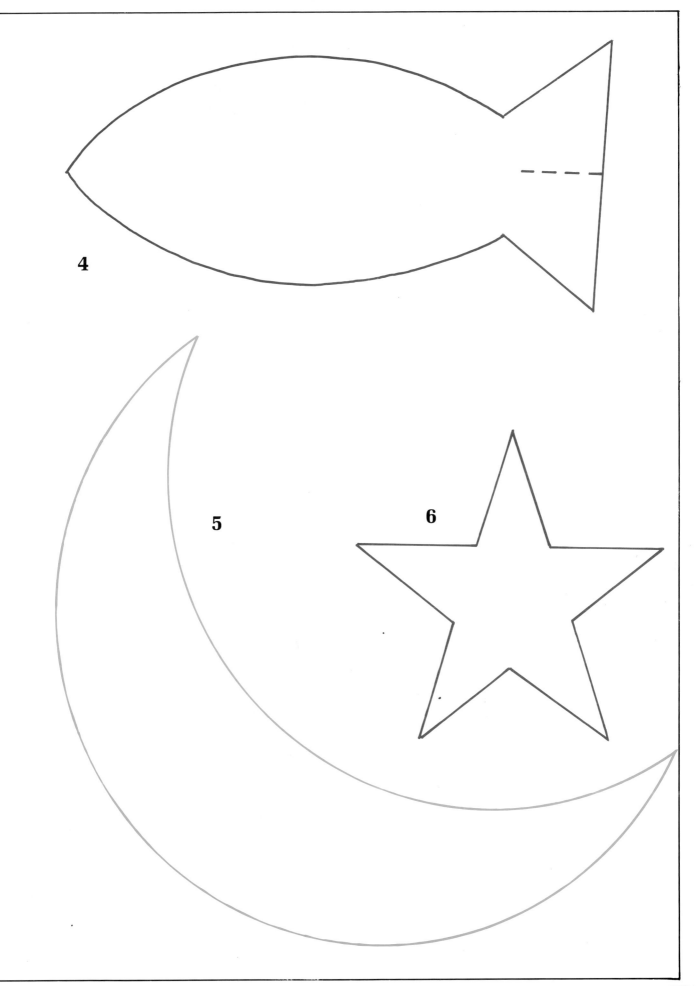

4

5

6

INDEX